There's a Mole in my Bucket

John Svatins

Published in 2024
by John Svatins

© Copyright John Svatins

ISBN: 978-1-913898-85-4

Illustrated by ©Izzy Svatins

Cover and Book interior Design
by Russell Holden
www.pixeltweakspublications.com

Pixel Tweaks Publications
SELF PUBLISHING MADE SIMPLE

For Connie and Izzy

It seems strange that daughter
Does not rhyme with laughter
They share most of the same letters
And both bring a smile to my face

CONTENTS

ANIMALS

O To Be An Octopus...1
Alphabetical Animals... 2
A Wolf's Tale 4
The Bird That Would Not Fly.............................. 8
Hippos 9
Dear Liza, A Mole! 10
I Saw a Polar Bear... 12
The Platypus 14

FAMILY

Heading North To See My Cousin...................... 19
When Daddy used the SatNav 20
Things My Great-Granny Says......................... 22
Revenge Of The Little Brother 24
Eating Sweets with My Sister In The Room 28
10 Things That Annoy Me 29
Uncle Darren Would Like To See The Manager...............30

FOOD

Worms for Tea 35
The Sorry Tale of Oliver Trott......................... 36
Swoop!... 39
Snacking With Sally.. 40
Chips, Cheese and Gravy................................. 42

FRIENDS

My Bighead Friend 47
My Mate... 48
Thank You.. 50
Making Friends 51
Try to be Lovely.. 52
Poem for my Enemy 53

NONSENSE

My Nonsense Poem..57
A Poet's Holiday..58
Scaredy Cat 60
The Good Ship Blubbernaut.......................................62
Body Doubles 64
Anagram Animals..66
Uncle Edgar..67
Compare the Wildebeest.com 68

PETS

Cattitude..73
My Rabbit Has A Habit 74
Mr Jamieson's Menagerie...75
Woof! 76

SCHOOL

Lessonitis...81
School Trip..82
Family Tree 84
Sports Day..86
My Football Is Inside The Cupboard 88
The Teacher's Disco...91

SPOOKY

Sweet Nightmares Are Made of This............................97
Skeletons Tell Terrible Jokes.....................................98
Veggie Peril 100
The Ghost of Fortune Street......................................102
Have a Spooky Christmas 105

10 Facts About John..109
About the Illustrator..111

ANIMALS

O To Be An Octopus

O, to be an octopus exploring ancient wrecks
Popping through their portholes
and sitting on their decks
A large exotic octopus with colour changing skin
That switches its appearance to match the mood I'm in
Or perhaps a tiny octopus that tickles swimmers' feet
Before it squirts to safety in the murky ocean's deep
I'd like to be an octopus with eight long arms or more
And communicate with divers in advanced semaphore
If I could be an octopus, I'd fill my days with leisure
Collect gold spoons, or count doubloons
from chests of sunken treasure
Why can't I be an octopus? I love their bulbous faces
And isn't it amazing that they fit in tiny spaces?
Please can I be an octopus? I won't kick up a stink
Unless of course you tread on me
and I cover you with ink
How I'd love to be an octopus, enjoying my safari
While dodging those Italians with a taste for calamari
Will I ever be an octopus? The chances seem remote
But if I do, I'll visit you and climb aboard your boat

Alphabetical Animals

Angry aardvarks argued, while
Blissful badgers beamed
Cunning camels cackled, as
Dozing donkeys dreamed

Emus eagerly escaped
From fearsome ferret foes
Giggling geckos gazed upon
Hyenas holding hoes

Ibex issued insults, to
Jealous jackal jerks
Kayaking koalas kissed, where
Loafing lizards lurked

Moody moles meandered
Near naughty nightingales
Old opossum ogled, and the
Prissy pandas paled

Quivering quokkas quaked before
Revolting rhino rumblings
Smirking sardines sniggered as
The tiny termites tumbled
Underfed umbrella birds
Vexed vivacious vermin
While wondrous weasels watched the
X-Ray tetra who was swimmin'

Yawning Yaks looked wistfully at
Zebras in their beds
And wondered at the way
They let out lines of hovering zeds

A Wolf's Tale

Once upon a hairy tale
(Yes, I got the spelling right)
A wolf stuck plasters on his fur
And moaned about his plight

For 5 long years he'd suffered
Since he was but a pup
From crafty pigs and girls in hoods
And now he was fed up

The vet said he had asthma
From blowing buildings down
And he thought he'd caught a case of fleas
From wearing grandma's gown

The last time he had eaten well
Was August or September
He thought he might have caught a slug
But couldn't quite remember

He longed to eat that girl in red
And her rotten granny too
Followed by a bacon roll
And a bowl of piggy stew

But thanks to Red and daddy's axe
His tail was now much shorter
And the pigs had scalded his behind
With a pan of boiling water

So wolfie went to search the web
From Instagram to Ebay
For something that would fill his tum
And make the rotters pay

His answer was to order up
A pizza (thin and crusty)
Delivered on a moped by
A spotty youth called Rusty

As Rusty reached the wolf's front door
The wolf leapt from the hall
And gobbled up the poor young man
Pizza box and all

So having finished off the boy
He took his coat and tie
And set of on the moped
For a certain piggy sty

Knock, knock went wolf upon the door
At the pig-house made of brick
"Pizza?" said the hopeful pig
And gave his lips a lick

But no one got to eat that night
Except our lupine friend
Who rounded up the piggies three
And brought about their end

With belly full of yummy pork
He got back on the moped
And up the road to grandma's house
The naughty wolf then sped

Alas, grandma was also fooled
By the pizza uniform
And the promise of a cheesy feast
With extra fries and corn

Thus satisfied, the wolf began
To wait for little Red
And feeling full of porky treats
He snoozed upon the bed

Some time had passed when Wolf awoke
The night had now turned black
"The moment's come for my revenge,
I'll have a midnight snack!"

His urge to eat Red Riding Hood
Blinded him from seeing
The visitor to Grandma's house
Was another furry being

No one knows poor Wolfie's fate
Although there's some who swear
That these days, when Red's in the wood,
She walks besides a bear

The Bird That Would Not Fly

As I plummeted down from my warm tree-top nest
I made the decision that walking was best
In a bird, such a thought may be reckoned profound
But it just seemed much safer to stay on the ground
My fine feathered siblings can swoop and can soar
But the future for me is down here on the floor
Does it matter if I select feet over flight?
It's warmer down here and I don't like the height
Up there you're exposed to the lightning and thunder
But down here there's always a bush to slip under
They can keep acrobatics and high altitude
I'll grub around here where there's plenty of food
They tell me it's easy to fly through the air
And say that I'd like it if only I'd dare
But I wonder if they have considered the threats
Of mid-air encounters with low flying jets
Or if they would think that their plumage was fine
Diced by the blades of a spinning turbine
Up there on the rooftops, they sneer and they scoff
But it's me that will laugh when the rotters fall off
Next week they're departing to find warmer weather
A synchronised lift-off of feathers together
They'll have to find some other bird to abuse
As I stroll to the docks and hop onto a cruise.

Hippos

It's said that hippopotamuses
Can weigh as much as minibuses
Despite this quite enormous size
A hippo rarely eats a pie
And though he'd eat your garden whole
He'll pass up on a sausage roll
Just as well 'cause on those legs
He'd never make it down to Greggs

Dear Liza, A Mole!

There's a mole in my bucket
dear Liza, dear Liza,
There's a mole in my
bucket, dear Liza, a mole

Then feed it an earthworm,
dear Henry, dear Henry
Then feed it an earthworm,
dear Henry a worm

There's a shark in my bathtub,
dear Liza, dear Liza
There's a shark in my bathtub, dear Liza, a shark

Then hand it the bath towel, dear Henry, dear Henry
Then hand it the bath towel, dear Henry, the towel

There's an owl in my teapot, dear Liza, dear Liza
There's an owl in my teapot, dear Liza, an owl

Then fill up the milk jug, dear Henry, dear Henry
Then fill up the milk jug, dear Henry, the jug

There's a crab in my wardrobe, dear Liza, dear Liza
There's a crab in my wardrobe, dear Liza, a crab

Then help put its pants on, dear Henry, dear Henry
Then help put its pants on, dear Henry, its pants

There's a bear in my bed now, dear Liza, dear Liza
There's a bear in my bed now, dear Liza a bear

That does it dear Henry, dear Henry, dear Henry
That does it, dear Henry, I'm moving next door

You're useless, dear Henry, dear Henry, dear Henry
You're useless, dear Henry. I hope the bear snores!

I Saw a Polar Bear

I saw a polar bear
WHERE?
THERE!
I saw a polar bear
WHERE?
THERE!
Underneath a chair
Munching on a pear
I saw a polar bear
WHERE?
THERE!

I saw a crocodile
WHERE?
THERE!
I saw a crocodile
WHERE?
THERE!
Hiding in the coats
Eating porridge oats
I saw a crocodile
WHERE?
THERE!

I saw an elephant
WHERE?
THERE!
I saw an elephant
WHERE?
THERE!
Sitting in the sink
Going for a drink
I saw an elephant
WHERE?
THERE!

I saw a kangaroo
WHERE?
THERE!
I saw a kangaroo
WHERE?
THERE!
Standing on your head
Chewing on some
bread
I saw a kangaroo
WHERE?
THERE!

I saw an octopus
WHERE?
THERE!
I saw an octopus
WHERE?
THERE!
Climbing up a tree
Eating KFC
I saw an octopus
WHERE?
THERE!

I saw a dinosaur
WHERE?
THERE!
I saw a dinosaur
WHERE?
THERE!
In my teacher's car
With a chocolate
bar
I saw a dinosaur
WHERE?
THERE!

I saw some animals
WHERE?
THERE!
I saw some animals
WHERE?
THERE!
Sitting in their places
Making scary faces
I saw some animals
WHERE?
THERE!

The Platypus

The platypus is small and shy
And keeps to waterways
They shun the busier places
Where other creatures play

You'll never find a platypus
Inside a forest clearance
Perhaps they're scared that wallabies
Will laugh at their appearance

It's true, the wondrous platypus
Resembles no one else
And looks like they were made up from
The bits left on the shelf

The usual choice for mammals
Is a trunk, a nose or snout
But platypuses have a bill
That's broad and sticks right out

And fluffy tail or smooth behind?
The platypus has neither
Instead this odd marsupial
Resembles most, a beaver

I promise this is all the truth
I wouldn't pull your leg
But little platypuses
Start their life off in an egg

And at his heel, the last surprise
A venom covered spike
To scare off curious naturalists
And others they dislike

I like the furry platypus
I hope they never change
For life would just be boring
If some of us weren't strange

FAMILY

Heading North To See My Cousin

My cousin's talking Scottish, I don't know what to do
When I look at a field of cows, she says she sees a coo
My cousin's talking Scottish, it may as well be Greek
I told her it was raining and she said that it was dreich
My cousin's talking Scottish, I s'pose that it's her habit
But should I be offended when she says I'm being crabbit?
My cousin's talking Scottish, I think she's going barmy
She said she had a piece for me, then handed me a sarnie
My cousin's talking Scottish, I hope it's not a joke
She told me fish is boggin and that sardines make her boak
My cousin's talking Scottish, I don't s'pose there's much harm
But I wish I could remember if a babe's a bairn or barn
My cousin's talking Scottish, and everything is wee
I know it seems a little thing, but it means a lot to me.

Translation for non-Scottish people!

Bairn – baby or young child
Boak – throw up
Boggin – disgusting
Coo – cow
Crabbit – bad tempered
Dreich – miserable wet weather
Piece – a sandwich
Wee – small

When Daddy used the SatNav

"There must be a shortcut," said Daddy one day
"Let's see if this app can suggest a new way."
So he tapped the screen of its glowing display
When Daddy used the SatNav

I thought it was strange that we drove through a stream
And still carried on when my mum gave a scream
Our trip to the shops had become a bad dream
When Daddy used the SatNav

The track that we took through a farm was quite fun
Till a man started shouting and waving his gun
I think that we drove through his new chicken run
When Daddy used the SatNav

The motorway journey made mummy distressed
The traffic was eastbound but we headed West
We decided that sticking to A roads was best
When Daddy used the SatNav

But we still carried on as Dad followed his guide
Ignoring us both as we sobbed and we cried
"A little bit further," was all he replied
When Daddy used the SatNav

The route that we followed became more bizarre
As we drove over tracks in our wandering car
Then onto a train with the sign, 'Eurostar'
When Daddy used the SatNav

The car became still as the train left the station
Whisking us off for an unplanned vacation
A voice said, "You've now reached your destination."
When Daddy used the SatNav

Things My Great-Granny Says

My great-gran's got some phrases
You'll only hear her say
I sometimes think she makes them up
Mum says it's just her way

"It was as black as Newgate's knocker
He's got ears like the F.A Cup
My stomach feels like my throats been cut
Your uncle's been banged up

My knees were wobbling like jelly
Her feet were two blocks of ice
Your aunties fought like rats in a sack
That's cheap at half the price

That boy's a bit peculiar
She's mad as a box of frogs
He looks like a bulldog chewing a wasp
That place has gone to the dogs

We couldn't rub tuppence together
My neighbour's as ugly as sin
She looks like mutton dressed as lamb
I'll take it on the chin"

I think she's speaking English
But sometimes have my doubts
I'm never absolutely sure
What she's been on about

I wonder if, when I am old
The kids will get confused
At things I'll chatter on about
Or phrases that I use

Great-great little children
Playing with a doll
Saying "Mummy, I just wet myself
And Grandpa John said 'Lol'"

Revenge Of The Little Brother

Our Tom strode in front of me
Wherever we would go
And would curse his little brother
For always being too slow

"Keep up," he'd yell behind him
While plunging on ahead
And I'd run to catch his lanky legs
'til my face was beetroot red

Then on a sweltering August day,
When other fun was had,
We chanced upon a creepy house,
That stopped this cocky lad.

"You go first," my brother said
And roughly pushed me on
His voice was cracked and trembling
The confidence was gone.

I scrambled up a plank of wood
We'd placed against the wall
And entered through a broken pane
Once shattered by a ball

The room inside was dusty
And the floorboards gave a creak
As I made my trembling progress
Too scared to shout or speak.

Tom squinted through the window
His face was white with fear
And seeing him so quiet and scared
Gave me a new idea.

I'd fix my moaning brother
Who treated me like dirt
I'd make him think again before
He called me little squirt!

So while my grumpy brother,
Was scrambling after me
I slipped into the hallway
To see what I could see

An armchair in the hallway
Was covered with a sheet
This would be amazing
Revenge, I thought, was sweet!

"Where are you James?" my brother called
His voice a tad uncertain
With sheet in hand, I formed a plan
And slipped behind a curtain

"Come back," he called, "It isn't safe"
As I took up my position
Just one more step and I'd leap out
A ghostly apparition

But stepping back to prime my jump
I met the cellar door
And crashed through wood and down the steps
Till I finally reached the floor

I don't recall the ambulance
And frankly, I don't care
But I'm told it took the fire brigade
To get me out of there

The first I knew about the fall
Was when I woke much later
Surrounded by my family
And a wheezing ventilator

The doctor said they'd keep me in
Till things were not so grim
My brother rolled his eyes at that
And my parents glared at him

"Not to worry though," they said
He'll soon be right as rain
And to keep them sympathetic
I gave a moan of pain

The nurse gave me some medicine
To take away my hurt
And as he left, my brother mouthed,
"You stupid little squirt!"

Eating Sweets With My Sister In The Room – Every time

Did you just steal a sweet from me?
I thought I had one more
I bet you pinched a strawberry one
When I went to answer the door
You did it again, I know you did
Just then, when I looked away
There's one less sweet and I'm sure it was you
I don't care what you say.
I'm telling mum, she'll sort you out
Did you think it wouldn't be missed?
You've taken another! I knew it was you
You've got them in your fist.
Return them all and I won't tell mum
I'll even close my eyes
You've taken the lot and disappeared!
Why am I not surprised?

10 Things That Annoy Me

Lilly's Diary

1) Homework
2) Getting dragged out on family walks
3) People who make noises when they eat
4) Spots
5) People who come in my bedroom without knocking
6) Boys who think it's funny to burp
7) Anyone apart from me picking on my brother
8) Parents!!!
9) Little brothers (see 3, 5 and 6)
10) Ella Hutchinson and her stupid haircut

TOM'S DIARY

1 BEING MADE TO GO TO WEDDINGS
2 BROCKLI
3 BEING LITTLE
4 HAVING TO GO TO BED BEFORE MY SISTER
5 ANYONE WHO IS NASTY TO MY SISTER – SMELLA HUTCHINSON!!!!
6 SPELLING TESTS
7 NOT GETTING PICKED FOR FOOTBALL
8 BEING BORED
9 LILLY WHEN SHE WON T PLAY WITH ME
10 PEEPLE MOANING ABOUT STUFF LIKE EATING WITH YOUR MOUTH OPEN

Uncle Darren Would Like To See The Manager

My Uncle Darren loves to moan
In person, text or on the phone
He makes himself a total pain
By finding reasons to complain

He shakes his fist and starts to shout
If kids should dare to stand about
And groups of softly spoken boys
Are tutted at for making noise

He yells at neighbours for their parking
Or if their dogs have started barking
He told the lady from next door
He didn't like the clothes she wore

In restaurants he'll choke and cough
To try and get some money off
And every single take-away
He'll try his hardest not to pay

It's almost like he takes a pride
In never being satisfied
And when he talks about the service
I find myself becoming nervous

He took some shoes back to the store
Because, 'They made his feet feel sore'
But only said they were too tight
To get some money off the price

He even made a long complaint
About a can of yellow paint
And said the price should be reduced
Because the lid was on too loose

He told a stranger at the gym
That sweaty men offended him
And tried to make the staff agree
To knock some money off his fee

I think he would become unhinged
If forced to go without a whinge
It seems that Darren's aim in life
Is spreading sorrow, pain and strife

My mum says that he's just demanding
And I should be more understanding
But Dad and me, we both agree
My uncle is a misery!

FOOD

Worms for Tea

I wonder whether earthworms
Are any good to eat
I wonder if they're sour
Or maybe sickly sweet

I wonder if they're tasty
Delicious, fine and scrummy
Or if they feel like rubber bands
Dissolving in your tummy

I s'pose that they're quite gritty
Given where they live
But cleaning them would not be hard
If you can find a sieve

I wonder if you ate one whole
And didn't chew the worm
If you'd feel it going down
And would you feel it squirm

The blackbirds seem quite fond of them
They eat them by the ton
So why would it be odd of me
To try a single one?

My brother thinks I'm horrible
But I think he's just petty
After all, I said to him
It's just like pink spaghetti

The Sorry Tale of Oliver Trott

This is the story of Oliver Trott
A vile, revolting child
Whose snacking made his mother ill
And drove his father wild

Manners for most, are simple things
Following them is easy
But what and how this creature ate
Made others feel quite queasy

Tinned sardines in custard sauce
Marshmallows served with gravy
To watch their son devour his tea
Would send his parents crazy

Earthworms roasted, woodlice grilled
Were treats for Master Trott
And when he found a mouldy cake
He promptly ate the lot

Knives and forks just slowed him down
With food he didn't linger
He'd rather use his hands like spades
Or skewer things on his finger

Lumpy milk bought months ago
He'd drink and smack his lips
Then rub the dandruff off his head
And sprinkle it on chips

And how, you ask, did Mr Trott
Put food upon his plate?
By rooting through the bins of course
For food well out-of-date

Spots, snot, assorted grot
Held no fear for Oliver Trott
And cheese that smelt like sweaty feet
He looked upon as quite the treat

His end was sadly quick and brief
The cause of it? A lettuce leaf
He never saw the salad lurking
While spreading jam upon a gherkin

Unbeknownst, he pushed it in
Then wiped some ketchup from his chin
He wheezed in pain, "I've been done in!
I think I ate a vitamin.

Of all the strange ingredients
They've finished me with nutrients!"
And then his face turned ashen grey
Poor Oliver had passed away.

This is the story of Oliver Trott
Who ate the food he found
And like the snacks he favoured most
He's rotting underground

Swoop!

Pizza and chips for tea
Mum says, 'None for me'
But we all know that's not true
'Cause she'll always pinch a chip or two
Then two becomes three or four
And soon a handful more
I don't know who to trust
When she nibbles at my crust
And you know she's never stopping
When she's picking at the toppings
Next she sips my Ribena
It's like living with a hyena!
'I can't seem to shift this weight'
She says as she grazes our plates
I just wish she'd eat her own meal
And she wasn't so tempted to steal
But mum thinks food like bacon
Tastes better when it's taken
And that food is calorie free
If she robs it off of me!

Snacking With Sally

Sally Parks ate anything
Post-it notes, bits of string
Pencil shavings and erasers
Buttons off your new school blazer
Gravel, pebbles, rocks and stones
Staplers, pens and mobile phones
Hair she pulled from Barbie dolls
Shampoo, soap and aerosols
Toilet paper off the roll
Bits of wood and lumps of coal
Chairs and tables, wardrobes too
Sellotape and tubes of glue
In school she ate a calculator
Followed by a radiator
"Get her out!" her teacher yelled
Before she swallowed him as well
Her mother said, "She's gone too far"
As Sally polished off their car
But mother's discontented grumbling
Was drowned by Sally's tummy rumbling
Gripped by the need for number twos
Sally retreated to the loo
The noise was deafening, the odour worse
Her parents sent out for a nurse
And minutes later, sirens wailing
An ambulance parked by the railings
The paramedics kept alert

They didn't want to be dessert
Police in tow they climbed the stair
To try and fix this sad affair
But then, without their intervention
A silence came from Sal's digestion
The toilet flushed, the door flung wide
"It's done!" said Sally full of pride
The nutty nosher staggered out
And standing tall she gave a shout
"My diet was most unbecoming
And sorry dad about the plumbing
I'll lay off eating household items
Or anything that tends to frighten
I'm sorry my teacher became a snack
(It's doubtful if we'll get him back)
But though I know the school feels sore
He really was an awful bore
From this day I'll follow a diet
That doesn't cause alarm
or riot
No more for me the household
features
Clothing, cars or pesky
teachers
Henceforth I'll keep my
range of meals
To normal things like
jellied eels"

Chips, Cheese and Gravy

Every chippy has a speciality that you can't get elsewhere. It might be a chicken parmo, a deep-fried pizza or orange chips. Where I live it's the wonderful chips, cheese and gravy. Your doctor won't thank you, but your stomach will!

You may be fond of Sunday roast
Or a slice of freshly buttered toast
But I know what I love the most
It's chips, cheese and gravy!

The combination might seems crazy
But just hang on and don't be hasty
Grab a plate, you'll see it's tasty
My chips and cheese and gravy

Some go wild for curry goat
Others like their nugs and Coke
But I'll leave that to other folk
I love chips, cheese and gravy!

You might regard my choices strangely
But I could eat it night and daily
It isn't posh, it isn't dainty
That chips and cheese and gravy!

Some like pizza, some like steak
Some the cakes their granny bakes
But I'll have what my chippy makes
It's chips, cheese and gravy!

Many think that chilli's good
And others opt for Yorkshire pud
But I want my choices understood
It's chips, cheese and gravy!

FRIENDS

My Bighead Friend

If he joined the army, we'd win every war
If he played for England, he'd probably score
If you won a medal, then he'd win four
He's an absolute pest
But he's sure he's the best

If he wrote a song it would be number one
If he lifted weights, he could bench press a ton
If he ran in a race, he would beat everyone
His tales are amazing
But eyebrow-raising

If you tell a joke, then he thinks his is better
If you got soaked he would say he was wetter
If you mention a singer, he'll tell you he's met her
I'm starting to suspect
His stories aren't correct

My Mate

Connor Franklin can burp out tunes
Takes pins to a party to burst balloons
Bangs on pans with serving spoons
Connor Franklin is great and he's my mate

Connor Franklin has a scar on his knee
He knows karate and says he'll teach me
He can get it highest when we go for a wee
Connor Franklin is great and he's my mate

Connor Franklin made a teacher cry
He can score a goal from the halfway line
His eyebrows don't move when he's telling a lie
Connor Franklin is great and he's my mate

Connor Franklin wears clothes that don't fit
And makes funny noises with his armpit
My sister says he's got the nits
Connor Franklin is great and he's my mate

Connor Franklin brings a Mars Bar for lunch
Made a hole in the ceiling with just one punch
When he eats soup he makes it crunch
Connor Franklin is great and he's my mate

Connor Franklin is our class clown
My mum says he lives in the rough part of town
His knees are a sort of muddy brown
Connor Franklin is great and he's my mate

Connor Franklin likes spiders and beetles
He keeps them in boxes then throws them at people
His uncle's in prison for something illegal
Connor Franklin is great and he's my mate

Connor Franklin has gone away
I asked my teacher, but she wouldn't say
I miss the games we used to play
Connor Franklin was great and he's still my mate

Thank You

Thanks for listening when I go on and on
Thanks for the sweets when I've got none
Thanks for playing games that no one else likes
Thanks for slowing down when we ride on our bikes
Thanks for not telling when I broke mum's mug
Thanks for being there when I need a hug
Thanks for staying up when we slept at my house
Thanks for not laughing when I screamed at the mouse
Thanks for smiling when I come in the room
Thanks for being patient when I say I'll be there soon
Thanks for forgetting when I make mistakes
Thanks for eating the things that I bake
I hope there are things that you're grateful for too
But I'm just thankful that I've got you.

Making Friends

Will you be my friend? I'll give you a sweet
I'll tell you some secrets you mustn't repeat
I'll let you sleep over if you'll be my mate
If you were my bestie, then things would be great

Will you be my friend? I'll join in your game
But not if it's dollies 'cause that's a bit lame
We could go to the woods and play hide and seek
I'll show you the tree that I climbed up last week

Will you be my friend? We can message online
If you tell me your username I'll tell you mine
Would you ask your mum if we could have tea?
I'm sure she'll say yes, once she gets to know me

Will you be my friend? I've got really good games
I'd play by myself, but it's just not the same
Is it alright if I come when you're walking home?
It's rubbish that sometimes I'm left on my own

Will you be my friend?
You will?
Oh, brill!

Try to be Lovely

Try to be lovely
Choose light over dark
The flame that brings warmth
Needs to start with a spark

It might be a word
Or a smile or a touch
The value is priceless
But doesn't cost much

The world's full of people
Who are feeling quite low
And the choices you make
Could help more than you know

So opt to act kindly
Encourage and comfort
Leave smugness to others
And hold back your judgement

We'll all have a time
When it's not going well
When events and mistakes
Bring their own private hell

It's then that you'll know
What the value of nice is
In helping you conquer
Your personal crisis

Try to be lovely
Choose light over dark
The flame that brings warmth
Needs to start with a spark

Poem for my Enemy

May your teddy bear's eyes be chewed off by the cat
and sicked-up in your dinner unnoticed.
May your brother draw pictures inside all your books
and your parents just yawn when you protest.

When you're eating your lunch with a glass of cold milk
I hope you get dust up your nose
So you sneeze out the lot at incredible speed
And it ends up all over your toes.

If you head for the loo when your family's asleep
May you tread on a hidden toy crane
And I hope that you're told off for screaming out loud
As you hop on the landing in pain.

Let an aunty with bad breath grab hold of your face
And kiss you again and again
Just when that girl from our class that you like
Walks past with all of her friends.

And I'll tell you the reason
I'm feeling this rage
So you don't think I'm having a whine.
You borrowed my felt tips
when I was away
And you left all the lids off,
you swine!

NONSENSE

My Nonsense Poem

Hogwash, balderdash, jibber jabber, guff

Claptrap, poppycock, made-up stuff

Piffle, blather, blarney, gibberish and tripe

Waffle, babble, bilge and prattle of all type

Gobbledygook, hot air, blether and rot

Craziness, stupidity, good sense – NOT!

Mumbo-jumbo, drivel, rubbish and baloney

Hooey and absurdity, What a lot of pony!

A Poet's Holiday

If I had a billion pounds
I'd take a world-wide trip
Experience the sights and sounds
And travel on a ship
But photographs and shopping
Would not take up my time
Instead my global hopping
Would be in search ... of rhymes

I'd paint myself green in Aberdeen
Throw a welly in New Delhi
Knit a jumper in Kuala Lumpa
Kick a ball round Montreal
Bang saucepan lids around Madrid
Make some jam in Amsterdam
Lie in a coma in Oklahoma
Cook a stew in Timbuctu
Play with Barbie in Abu Dhabi
Open a door in Singapore
Buy a spanner in Havana
Eat baked beans in New Orleans
Use a hoover in Vancouver
Eat something stinky in Helsinki
Learn guitar in Bogata
Chase a turkey in Alburquerque
Sing 'Let it Go' in Tokyo
Drive a gorilla around Manilla
And snap a stick in Rekjavik

Then after 30 years or more
Of travelling round the earth
Of making verses shore to shore
From Port au Prince to Perth
I'd sail away and spend the rest
Of my remaining time
On a pretty little island
With a name that doesn't rhyme!

Scaredy Cat

I'm scared of men that have big beards
The bushy ones the most
And shiver at the thought they might
Be hiding bits of toast.
If I should see a magpie perched
Upon my apple tree
I'm terrified that something bad
Will soon occur to me.
For others, thirteen holds no fear
They hardly bat an eye
but if I meet that dread amount
I'm sure that I will die.
At night I keep the light switched on
And lock my cupboard door
For fear that loathsome monsters
Will grab me with their claws.
I'm scared of creatures with eight legs
And six and four and two
Which can make things quite awkward
When I'm visiting the zoo.
I'm not too keen on travelling
By boat or car or train
And cannot even contemplate
A journey in a plane.

I even fear the phobias
That haven't yet got names
And dread an unknown horror
I really can't explain.
In fact, the list of things that add
To my anxiety
Is pretty much unlimited
As far as I can see.
But worse than beards or snakes or heights
Or beasts that snarl and drool
Is the thought that one day, I might be
A teacher in a school.

The Good Ship Blubbernaut

Climb aboard the Blubbernaut
We're off to sail the seas
In a ship that has more holes in it
Than a slice of mouldy cheese
Our sailors are all fearless
A brave and hardy crew
Alas it's not just fear they lack
They're also brainless too

Climb aboard the Blubbernaut
And see the seven oceans
Catch scurvy, plague or get a rash
Impervious to lotions
We fly the skull and mobile phones
Not quite what you'd expect
We'll rob you of your booty
And then send a nasty text

Climb aboard the Blubbernaut
And serve with Captain Bones
They say he's sunk a dozen ships
Nine of them his own
Sing shanty songs and practise knots
While lost in the Pacific
Get shipwrecked with some cannibals
Or something more horrific

Climb aboard the Blubbernaut
Steal treasure that's been cursed
You'll probably get back to port
If the rats don't eat you first
Say goodbye and sail away
Take up your pirate sword
For there's no hope of going back
Once you have stepped aboard

Body Doubles

The patient at the doctor's,
was feeling rather strange
So he set out all his
symptoms,
their severity and range.
Though his illness might
confuse you
I'll report it faithfully
And give his words exactly
As they were told to me.

"I need to share my secret,
to get this off my knee,
I hope that we'll see nose to nose
and you'll agree with me.
It's making me cry my toes out
and costs me a foot and an arm.
Please stick out your bum and lend me a thumb
Before I come to harm.

It started when I was knocked over
By a terrier chasing his ball
I went foot over ear, landed flat on my head
And was dazed and confused by the fall.
I tried to have words with the owner
I was angry, in fact my skin boiled
But my thoughts felt twisted, my efforts ham-wristed
And the words that came out were all spoiled.

'Be brave,' said my mum, 'best rib forwards,
take liver, and earlobe your troubles.'
But I struggle to get my neck round it
And each day my confusion just doubles.
You've got to help me doctor
I can't armpit it any more
I can see you're all teeth, please give me relief
And make things as they were before."

The doctor peered over her glasses,
and got to the problem at hand
Setting out for her patient, quite simply
The restorative treatment she planned
"Take three chapters a day from a novel
learn a language, perhaps French or Russian
and we'll try to correct the impairment
that's afflicted you since your concussion.

But don't be down-hearted, chin up.
I'm sure that we'll soon have you fixed
If you follow the cure I've advised,
Your idioms should come unmixed.
It's the fault of that dog's careless owner,
Such behaviour is simply outrageous,
He ought to have kept his dog to leg

Oh no! I think you're contagious!"

Anagram Animals

Do **hornets** sit on royal **thrones**?

Do **tunas** call their **aunts** on phones?

Do **owls** go **slow** for miles and miles?

Are **soccer idols, crocodiles**?

A **horse** that canters on the **shore**

Could meet an **otter** eating **torte**

But **goats** in **togas**? Surely not

A **wasp** with **paws**, he'd sooner spot

Do **apes** eat chicken, rice and **peas**?

Is **false** the word that sums up **fleas**?

Ocelots may be the **coolest**

But can they **tutor trout** as students?

The **nicest insect** sees no gain

In watching while a **snail** is **slain**

And **rats** that **star** in films and plays

Sneak snake-like off on holiday

Uncle Edgar

Poor Uncle Edgar was just a little strange
He bought a bow and sparrow
For shooting on the range

Poor Uncle Edgar was frankly quite bizarre
He cut his toenails once a month
And kept them in a jar

Poor Uncle Edgar could be a little weird
He had a giant millipede
That lived inside his beard

Poor Uncle Edgar was really very odd
He told the local fishmonger
That he believed in cod

Poor Uncle Edgar was practically unique
He travelled to Uzbekistan
But only spoke in Greek

Poor Uncle Edgar was funny in the head
He thought that he could learn to fly
And now poor Edgar's dead

Compare the Wildebeest.com

A meerkat from the Kalahari
Saved up and bought a red Ferrari
He drove it over desert dunes
While whistling ancient meerkat tunes
Driving fast, he headed east
But hit a travelling wildebeest
The slowly moving ruminant
Gave out a quite frustrated grunt
"You idiotic furry clown
You really ought to slow it down"
And looking at the red car's bonnet
He promptly placed his rump upon it
The sportscar's delicate suspension
Experienced a heightened tension
And with a noise that broke his heart

The meerkat's sportscar fell apart
The meerkat wailed, "Your fat backside
Has just destroyed my awesome ride"
The wildebeest just slowly turned
Displaying not the least concern
"The fault is yours for this occurrence
I hope you've got some good insurance"
And with a snort and haughty cough
The wildebeest then wandered off
The meerkat cried, the meerkat wailed
The colour of his fur coat paled
For as he'd recently discovered
He couldn't get insurance cover
His treatment had been most unfair
From Direct Line to Go Compare
The companies had rudely snubbed
His payment made in worms and grubs
Despite the adverts that you see
They don't sell meerkats policies

PETS

Cattitude

My cat just sits around all day
She doesn't even want to play
And when we offer gentle kisses
She backs away and loudly hisses
To treat her once, I fed her kipper
She left a 'present' in my slipper
Sometimes, sitting on my knee
She tries to sink her claws in me
I've tried and tried to make her purr
This grumpy ball of orange fur
But in return for my affection
She gives me nothing but rejection
I know it's mean to say,
and yet
I wish we'd bought a
different pet

My Rabbit Has A Habit

My rabbit has a habit
He twitches his whiskers and sniffs the air
Chews holes in the socks I wanted to wear
He turns his head and licks his fur
Then he curls in my lap to take a nap

My rabbit has a habit
He hides behind sofas and under chairs
He covers the carpet in fine white hairs
He waits in the hall when I go upstairs
He looks at a book for ages, then chews the pages

My rabbit has a habit
He has a snack about half past two
Then goes in a corner to pop out some poos
It's always dozens, never a few
It drives my sister mad, but they really don't smell bad

My rabbit has a habit
When I'm sitting on my bedroom floor
Of using his head to open the door
Then climbing on me with furry paws
I'm not making an objection, I love his soft affection

My rabbit has a habit
When he's in the deepest slumber
He dreams of carrots without number
Of lettuce, mangetout and cucumber
He's a fiend for food that's green, a salad eating machine

Mr Jamieson's Menagerie

Well Mr Jamieson, we've come to your address

Because the neighbours have complained

about the noise and mess

That'll be the dogs you say, seventeen in all?

And probably the twenty cats sitting on that wall

What other pets do you have sir, living in your house?

A sheep, three goats, a donkey, a lizard and a mouse!

What do you mean, 'A monkey too'?

That surely can't be true

'It lives beside the wallaby, inside the downstairs loo'!

What about the smell sir? Did you ever think,

To open up your windows? Your house must surely stink!

What d'you mean, 'You can't do that,

the birds would fly away'?

That's enough, it's time to call, the RSPCA!

Woof!

Sid the dog protects me, he sees danger everywhere
Hiding in the cupboards or underneath a chair
Tucked behind the sofa, up a drainpipe spout
Sid detects invaders he must tell us all about
While others trust security, I use an angry pet
Who spends his life convinced
that every visitor's a threat
Royal Mail and Amazon even UPS
Are given vocal notice he stands
guard at this address
He scares off fearsome creatures,
like blackbirds in the tree
And keeps me safe
from dogs and cats appearing on TV
Before I tuck him in his bed
he goes to check the yard
Where Sid will pace from side to side
patrolling like a guard
With rumbling growls he keeps me safe
from other dogs we meet
And lord forbid a van should beep,
reversing up the street
At sounds unheard by human ear
my little sentry whines
Alerted by a squirrel's step
his furry head inclines

I can't call Sid a naughty boy but
he's not a dog messiah
Thanks to him I've now become
the neighbourhood pariah
But I'll survive if others
think of me as less attractive
They've never had to share a house
with someone so reactive
The grumbles and complaints
are fairly easy to ignore
Because my dog barks loudest
when he greets me at the door.

SCHOOL

Lessonitis

I'm angry with art and fed up of Spanish
Frankly I wish that DT would just vanish
Computing is cringe and PE makes me sick
History and Geography get on my wick
English is driving me slowly insane
RE is causing me physical pain
I wish that mathematics could just disappear
And PSHE makes me shiver in fear
Music is maddening, science is worse
There isn't a subject I don't want to curse
But still they keep sending me back to the school
            A treatment I think is
                  exceptionally cruel
                  My mood is sinking ever
                        deeper
                        Why did I choose to
                        be a teacher?

School Trip

Going on a school trip, leaving class behind
We're missing loads of lessons, but I don't mind

Going on a school trip, the coach will leave at nine
I bet Katrina misses it, she never comes on time

Going on a school trip, fighting over seats
Pulling faces at the cars we pass along the street

Going on a school trip passing sweets around
Lola tried to reach for one and got told to sit down

Going on a school trip, half of us feel ill
Mum bought me some medicine, but I forgot to
take the pill

Going on a school trip, finally we're there
I'm not sure where we've ended up, but no one
seems to care

Going on a school trip, it's actually quite good
There's models with their heads cut off and lots
guts and blood

Going on a school trip, we've stopped so we can eat
I've got peanut butter sandwiches and biscuits
for a treat

Going on a school trip they showed us lots of stuff
I tried to talk to Lola, but she went off in a huff

Going on a school trip, piling in the shop
Gracie got two rubbers and she says she'll do a swap

Going on a school trip, pile back on the bus
Tina's lost the pen she bought and starts to
make a fuss

Going on a school trip, it's not as noisy as before
Till Freddie Smith falls off to sleep and gently starts
to snore

Going on a school trip, we pull up at the gates
There's parents checking watches 'cause we're twenty
minutes late

We've all been on a school trip, I'd go back if I could
I can't remember much we did, but the other bits
were good

Family Tree

'For homework this week,' Miss Shaw told the class,
You'll be making a family tree
Talk to your relatives, write it all down
And return it by Monday to me

So Kelly got started with ruler and pens
Recording each adult and child
She rang aunties and uncles to check on the facts
And by Monday the work was compiled.

On a wallpaper roll that was bigger than her
She'd set out each generation
And she'd joined them all up with precision and care
To show marriages, deaths and relations

"My mum's in a heart above me and my sis
I've written my brother in too
My dad and his girlfriend are there
at the edge
But in pencil because she's quite new.

Holly, my cousin, is written in pink
With a circle of yellow stars
I've got other cousins like
Megan and Tom
But Holly's my favourite by far

84

I've got two real aunties called Jenny and Sue
I've written their names out in pen
In pencil are aunties who work with my mum
And people we see now and then

Dad's brother Micky still visits sometimes
And he helps out when something needs done
I once heard my mum say to her sister Sue
That she probably picked the wrong one.

I've tried to connect us with arrows or lines
In the corner I've written a key
Except for my guinea-pigs Wiggles and Bob
'Cos they're not related to me.

Sports Day

First of all the sack race and they're ready on the line
Henry's got a hole in his but says that he'll be fine
Then the whistle goes and they start bouncing in their sacks
Except for Henry in the lead, who's running down the track

Next of all the egg and spoon but things are quickly spoiled
When everyone discovers that the eggs have not been boiled
Sticky mess goes everywhere, it really is no joke
Especially for the teachers that were splatted with the yolk

Time to start the welly throw and boots are handed out
"Careful how you throw them," says the teacher with a shout
Through the air, the rubber boots get flung in all directions
Making parents run away to look for some protection

Then the teachers line the track with nets and hoops
and cones
Anticipation fills the crowd and parents raise their phones
The obstacles are all laid out, the race will soon begin
With seven nervous infants, all hoping they will win

The whistle goes, the children start and everybody yells
Past the cones, then through the hoops and things
are going well
But soon disaster strikes and all the teachers feel regret
Seven screaming infants who are tangled in a net!

Then everybody lines up for the final sports day races
Parents look on nervously as children take their places
Emily leads Baljeet and is surely going to win
When Baljeet's dog runs on the field determined to join in

Emily and Baljeet's dog collide and both go flying
Baljeet tries to catch his dog and Emily starts crying
Everyone gets stickers and the parents give a clap
Then Baljeet's dog escapes again to run a victory lap

The competition's over and the children get a snack
Tired bodies lie around the field and running track
It isn't clear who won the day, but no one seems to care
It all went slightly bonkers but they'll do it all next year

My Football Is Inside The Cupboard

(To the tune of 'My Bonny Lies Over The Ocean')

My football is inside the cupboard
My football has been locked away
My football is inside the cupboard
And I've got no football to play

I just brought it in for the breaktime
We like a good match after work
I don't know why that was a problem
Or why teacher went so berserk

Bring back, bring back
Bring back my footie to me, to me
Bring back, bring back
Oh bring back my footie to me

It started when she left the classroom
And I went to check on my ball
I'm not sure how it left my rucksack
But now it was out in the hall

My friend saw the ball on the carpet
And asked me to give him a go
I knew that I'd kicked it too firmly
The moment it left my big toe

Bring back, bring back
Bring back my footie to me, to me
Bring back, bring back
Oh bring back my footie to me

It entered the class like a rocket
And smacked my friend Tom on the nose
Then rebounded on towards Ella
Who headed it to the back row

Then everyone scrambled to join in
And tables were pushed out the way
A goal was set up at the bookcase
And everyone started to play

Bring back, bring back
Bring back my footie to me, to me
Bring back, bring back
Oh bring back my footie to me

The game was quite short but exciting
I think that the score was three-one
I don't know who shattered the whiteboard
But everyone had lots of fun

After it bounced off a laptop
I tried for an overhead pass
I managed to make a connection
And that's when the window got smashed

Bring back, bring back
Bring back my footie to me, to me
Bring back, bring back
Oh bring back my footie to me

The classroom was suddenly silent
And everyone turned to the door
Where Teacher stood looking like thunder
At me and my lovely football

She looked at the glass on the carpet
She looked at the blood on Tom's face
And then without giving a reason
She took my poor football away

Bring back, bring back
Bring back my footie to me, to me
Bring back, bring back
Oh bring back
my footie to me

The Teacher's Disco

The lights go down, the music starts
And dancing like your dad
Comes a dressed-up Mr Johnson
Looking, frankly, sad.
He's joined by Mr Williams
Who's moving to the beat
Which can be quite a challenge
With size eleven feet

They're dancing very badly
Their clothes are far too tight
There're teachers at the disco
And they're staying out all night

Mrs Davies joins the men
And does her cha cha slide
Then beckons Mrs Baker
Who tried her best to hide.
Mrs D grabs Mrs B
the better to persuade her
To join the fun and show them all
Her famous Macarena

They're dancing very badly
Their clothes are far too tight
There're teachers at the disco
And they're staying out all night

Mrs Robertson cries out,
"Look out, it's the boss
As their very own headteacher
Begins to do her floss.

Her elbows catch a waiter
And knocks the poor chap down
Showering soup on Mrs Singh
and mash on Mr Brown

They're dancing very badly
Their clothes are far too tight
There're teachers at the disco
And they're staying out all night.

Mrs Hussain hums a tune
Miss Thomas sings along
It's such a shame that both of them
Have picked a different song.
Mr Evans tries his best
To fix the dreadful wailing
But the two of them sound like a boy
Whose head's stuck in the railings.

They're dancing very badly
Their clothes are far too tight
There're teachers at the disco
And they're staying out all night.

Mr Khan swings Mrs Bond
Who's screaming fit to burst
But lets her go and off she flies
to land on Mrs Hearst.
Mrs Hearst then staggers back
Into the DJ's lap
He smiles and says he doesn't mind
So she gives his cheek a slap

They're dancing very badly
Their clothes are far too tight
There're teachers at the disco
And they're staying out all night.

Skidding on the dancefloor
Sliding on his knees
Mr Taylor makes his entrance
By flattening Mrs Lee.
Mrs Lee lets fly a punch
To land on Taylors's jaw
But misses him and hits instead
Unfortunate Miss Shaw.

They're dancing very badly
Their clothes are far too tight
There're teachers at the disco
And they're staying out all night.

The trouble-making teachers
Are thrown out of the club
And some decide to head for home
(With a quick stop at the pub)
Their backs are sore and aching
Their joints are full of pain
But still they think it's worth it
Just to be young again.

They're dancing very badly
Their clothes are far too tight
The teachers have left the disco
It's time to say goodnight.

SPOOKY

Sweet Nightmares Are Made of This
(To the tune of 'Favourite things')

20-foot ferrets with head-mounted lasers
Disgruntled vampires with teeth sharp as razors
Half-eaten maggots you find in your cake
These are the nightmares that keep me awake

Armies of blood-thirsty kangaroo robots
Going to Greggs and they've sold out of doughnuts
Tentacled monsters that lurk in the deep
Live in the nightmares I get when I sleep

Ninja trained squirrels or hedgehog assassins
Needing a wee when you're stuck in the traffic
Crashing to Earth from a mind-boggling height
Fill up my head if I turn out the light

If I doze off
If I cat-nap
If I fall asleep
I know that I'm in for a nasty surprise
As soon as I close, my eyes!

Skeletons Tell Terrible Jokes

Zombies shuffled aimlessly with heads tipped to one side
The phantoms rattled chains and flung transparent cloaks
out wide
The vampires swooped theatrically as they are wont to do
And ghoulish forms materialised in pools of dripping goo

"Wait everyone," the skeleton interrupted, *"I've got a joke*

Spectres paled spectacularly, their colour swiftly drained
Ghosts gave agonising moans evoking thoughts of pain
Frankenstein looked stoney-faced and gnashed
uneven teeth
And through the soil a groan was heard from things
that lie beneath

"No, don't be like that, it's really good!

Apparitions looked around for somewhere to escape
Vlad the Prince of Darkness huddled underneath his cape
Lost souls tried to lose themselves and ended up confused
While werewolves asked with urgency if they could be
excused

"Why ..." began the skeleton with an excessively toothy grin,
" can't I go to the party?"

Things from fevered nightmares screamed that they had
had enough
Spooks that had the talent disappeared with just a puff
Desperate sobs were heard from every supernatural being
All wishing they were capable of joining those yet fleeing

"Because I haven't got an invitation!"
"Hang on, that's not it ....."

The skeleton was glared at by a thousand bloodshot eyes
And heads intact and severed were all
shaken with a sigh
"It seems," a wraith hissed softly, "that
it isn't just a rumour,
Those without a body have a
lousy sense of humour"

Veggie Peril
WARNING – This poem is grisly!!

Billy Hearst of Clarence Street
Decided that he'd give up meat
And so next week he spent a while
Shopping in the grocery aisle
Unbeknownst to Mr Hearst
The veg he got had all been cursed

The crop he bought so eagerly
Had quite the chequered history
Grown by witches gripped with mania
Then flown by plane from Transylvania
Who could guess such evil dwelt
Upon the supermarket shelf?

And later, by his kitchen pans
The veggies made their awful plans
Keen to settle up a score
With every single herbivore
Bewitched by cruel and unhinged minds
To take revenge for veggie kind

Back from work, came poor young Bill
Unaware that veg can kill
Fooled by blogs and recipes
To hunger after rice and peas
He didn't note the deathly quiet
Of his deadly plant-based diet

Billy opened up the door
And veggies poured across the floor
In the front of the attack
Came onions bursting from their pack
Followed a pair of spuds
Crying out for Billy's blood

Soon the lad was overpowered
By broccoli and cauliflower
His hair was pulled, his shirt was torn
By a really not sweetcorn
And savage kicks were handed out
By scores of angry Brussel sprouts

He struggled in the mighty grip
Of pumpkins and entranced parsnips
Carrots, radish and cucumber
Added to the vengeful number
Then Billy's head was squashed between
A pair of cackling aubergines

His end – a kind of horrid joke
Was death by way of artichoke
Starved of air, he met his doom
Watched by freshly picked mushrooms
Poor Billy Hearst had ceased to be
Destroyed by veggie sorcery

And when detectives searched the scene
The vegetables could not be seen
They all escaped without detection
And went back to the fresh food section
We don't know if they'll ever stop
So just take care when you next shop!

The Ghost of Fortune Street

I am the ghost of Fortune Street
Your local Primary
My grave was in an open field
Then they built a school on me.

For centuries I was content
To glide behind the ploughs
Or if I felt some devilment
To agitate the cows

It wasn't much, I will admit
To keep this spirit up
Spooking pigs or making sounds
To scare the farmyard pup

But then the farm was boarded up
And builders started working
Which gave me endless ways that I
Could polish up my lurking

I annoyed a trainee carpenter
By undoing all his screws
Then made him fall by tying up
The laces on his shoes

The plumber got a nasty fright
While looking down a hole
As I popped out and yelled, "Beware,
I'm coming for your soul!"
But slightly later than they planned
The primary school was finished
And thus thought I, my spooking days
Will now be quite diminished

How wrong I was, I'm pleased to say
My fun had only started
Who knew that death could be so good
For those who have departed?

Gluing up the scissors
Scribbling in a book
Stuffing someone's jumper
Where I know they'll never look

Making farting noises
When the teacher crouches down
Hiding all the colours
So you're only left with brown

Waiting till the teacher's cross
And she has called for quiet
Then tickling random children
So I nearly cause a riot

Emptying a lunchbox
Knocking over drinks
Causing floods in bathrooms
With a plug stuck in the sink

I can't remember when I felt
So happy and alive
Amazing since I passed away
In 1825

I think I'll hang around the place
And do more of the same
I like it most when I've been bad
And others get the blame

The teachers keep discussing
Why behaviour's bad in school
They don't suspect that most of it
Is committed by a ghoul

But in the office yesterday
As I gave a ghostly wail,
The secretary got a call
That made her turn quite pale

The school is to be visited
By a man called an inspector
This could be fun, I wonder if
He's ever met a spectre?

Have a Spooky Christmas or
I Think I Need A New Boyfriend

On the first day of Christmas, my true love sent to me, the scream of an Irish banshee

On the second day of Christmas, my true love sent to me, two bogeymen and the scream of an Irish banshee

On the third day of Christmas, my true love sent to me, three phantom cats, two bogeymen and the scream of an Irish banshee

On the fourth day of Christmas, my true love sent to me, four hungry trolls, three phantom cats, two bogeymen and the scream of an Irish banshee

On the fifth day of Christmas, my true love sent to me, FIVE SEVERED HEADS! Four hungry trolls, three phantom cats, two bogeymen and the scream of an Irish banshee

On the sixth day of Christmas, my true love sent to me, six evil spirits, FIVE SEVERED HEADS! Four hungry trolls, three phantom cats, two bogeymen and the scream of an Irish banshee

On the seventh day of Christmas, my true love sent to me, seven shuffling zombies, six evil spirits, FIVE SEVERED HEADS! Four hungry trolls, three phantom cats, two bogeymen and the scream of an Irish banshee

On the eighth day of Christmas, my true love sent to me, eight ghosts a-groaning, seven shuffling zombies, six evil spirits, FIVE SEVERED HEADS! Four hungry trolls, three phantom cats, two bogeymen and the scream of an Irish banshee

On the ninth day of Christmas, my true love sent to me, nine witches flying, eight ghosts a-groaning, seven shuffling zombies, six evil spirits, FIVE SEVERED HEADS! Four hungry trolls, three phantom cats, two bogeymen and the scream of an Irish banshee

On the tenth day of Christmas, my true love sent to me, ten cauldrons bubbling, nine witches flying, eight ghosts a-groaning, seven shuffling zombies, six evil spirits, FIVE SEVERED HEADS! Four hungry trolls, three phantom cats, two bogeymen and the scream of an Irish banshee

On the eleventh day of Christmas, my true love sent to me, eleven vampires swooping, ten cauldrons bubbling, nine witches flying, eight ghosts a-groaning, seven shuffling zombies, six evil spirits, FIVE SEVERED HEADS! Four hungry trolls, three phantom cats, two bogeymen and the scream of an Irish banshee

On the twelfth day of Christmas, my true love sent to me, twelve wailing werewolves, eleven vampires swooping, ten cauldrons bubbling, nine witches flying, eight ghosts a-groaning, seven shuffling zombies, six evil spirits, FIVE SEVERED HEADS! Four hungry trolls, three phantom cats, two bogeymen and the scream of an Irish banshee

10 Facts About John

(1 is made up but the other 9 are more or less true)

1) He has two daughters
2) John has been searched by a policeman twice and on both occasions, he was carrying a boiled egg
3) He can juggle up to six balls at once
4) His dog Sid cuddles up on the sofa and then makes terrible smells
5) When John makes terrible smells, he blames it on Sid
6) He has taught over 1000 children
7) His dad came from Latvia
8) John has received letters addressed to Mr Sweetins, Mr Sweatins and Mrs Vatins
9) His sisters once tied him to a chair to practise their makeup on him
10) John once ate a spider by mistake

You can find more of John's poems and stories at:
www.somethingthatiwrote.co.uk
If you go there, you can also find details of how to get John to visit your school!

About the Illustrator

Izzy lives in Cumbria when she isn't in Liverpool training to be a radiotherapist.
She loves gaming, painting and baking instead of getting work done. Her artistic influences include Peanuts cartoons, the Beano and random internet memes.

You can find more of her art @Platypusafro on Instagram and Tiktok.

9 781913 898854